Lessons on Demonology

Volume 1

BISHOP COURTNEY MCLEAN

PUBLISHED BY:

Jamaica, W.I .

ISBN 978-976-96708-9-1

Cover Designed by: Geek Resource Centre
(geekjamaica@gmail.com)

Edited by: DMS Research, Editing & Documentation Services
dmscoachingandeditingservices@gmail.com
Telephone #: 1-876-919-7976

Published by: Yahweh's Anointed Publishing
Tel: 876-549-0063/876-438-2256
Email: yahwehsanointedpublishing@gmail.com
Website: https://yapublishing.com

PREFACE

The topic of Demonology is one that can never be exhausted. In my years of study,

I have found numerous avenues one can travel when researching this topic. Theologians have looked at this topic from several vantage points some of which are included here.

This manual contains my thoughts and understanding on the topic following years of experience and encounters with the supernatural. It is designed to provide a basic understanding of the topic to Christians who are interested in learning/exploring this topic.

TABLE OF CONTENTS

INTRODUCTION

A few years ago after I finished preaching in a powerful service, I went to the office to refresh myself and prepare to leave as I was extremely tired. My day had started really early and it was now almost midnight.

When I exited the office doors, I saw a car careening down the church's driveway at high speed. All eyes were on it as it came to a stop close to the church's door. I watched as a man and a woman struggled to pull a young girl out of the car. The young girl was hysterical. One person was holding both legs, while the other person was holding the upper part of her body.

As I looked on, I heard this strange language coming from the mouth of the young girl. Her mother was crying and shouted as she came towards me, *"Bishop, please help my daughter. She is demon possessed!"*.

The young girl appeared to have little or no control over her body. The ferociousness in her eyes was startling. She hurled insults and threats to everyone around while gyrating her body in a sexual manner. It was clear that this young girl was overtaken by demons. In order to help her, I interviewed the mother to identify what types of spirits were manifesting through her and to ascertain how they entered. Her mother explained that her daughter was only fourteen years old.

She recently found out that her daughter was staying up late at nights to watch pornography on the internet. Not only was she watching pornography but she was also engaging in the sexual acts she was seeing. Her mother was not able to say with certainty how long her daughter had been watching pornography but felt it might have been for a while based on when she started noticing changes in her behaviour. It also appeared that she might have been sexually active given the level of sexual hunger she was demonstrating. Hearing that, my team and I went to work. It took about three hours before all the spirits came out of her. Glory to God. She was delivered.

Satan and his cohorts are spiritual beings who wage war continuously against God, the holy angels, and humanity. As Christians, we cannot ignore the fact that demons do exist and are desperately seeking to enter our bodies and take control of our lives. From the story above we learned that when we have any kind of open doors in our lives, we create the opportunity for demons to enter. This book seeks to educate us on what the Bible teaches about demons, and how they operate. This is called *Christian demonology.*

Christian demonology focuses on the study of demons and their operations from a biblical point of view. Every firm Believer or Christian should have basic knowledge of demonology. Such information helps us to be aware of Satan, his minions, and their evil schemes. In order to fully understand the term demonology, it is, therefore, necessary to first understand the world in which we live and the spirits which operate in each realm.

Before you read this book, pray and ask God to cover you and your family as you seek to educate yourself on demonology. Additionally, ask God to open your mind to be able to comprehend and apply the information within to live well and be able to serve the kingdom of God.

PART 1

ORIGINS OF DEMONS

Observation of the Holy Scriptures vaguely gives reference to the origin of demons. Irrespective of the fact that we do not know their origin, we are absolutely certain that demons do exist, and most importantly, they must be confronted and expelled. We have seen many examples in the Bible where Jesus not only cast out demons out of individuals but He also empowered His disciples to do the same.

Two theological viewpoints regarding the origin of demons will be explored 1 below: *the Nephilim and the Pre-Adamic Race.*

THEOLOGICAL VIEWPOINTS

The Nephilim's

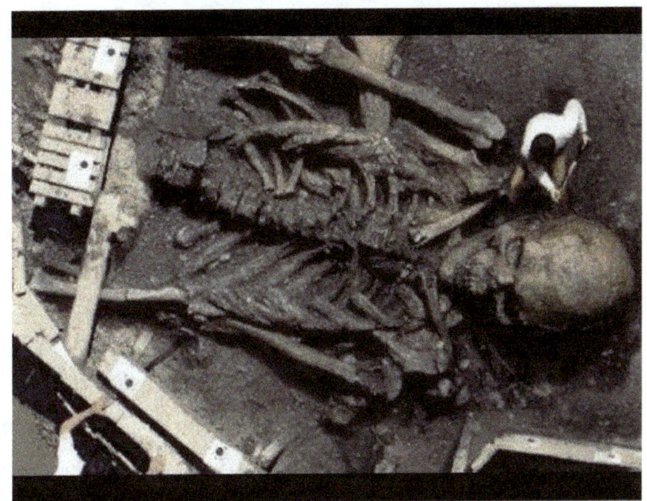

Published December 21, 2011 https://www.youtube.com/watch?v=YvkWZRlXgQE

Nephilim means "fallen ones". The word can be found in Genesis 6, Ezekiel 32, and Numbers 13. The Nephilim were giants. They were the violent superhuman offsprings produced when wicked angels mated with human women in the days of Noah as recounted in **Genesis 6:2, "***That the sons of God saw the daughters of men that they were fair; and they took them wives of all which they chose.*" Those 'sons of God' were actually spirit creatures who rebelled against God when they "*forsook their own proper dwelling place*" in heaven, materialized in human bodies, and "*began taking as wives all whom they chose.*"

> *And the angels which kept not their first estate, but left their own habitation, he hath reserved in everlasting chains under darkness unto the judgment of the great day.* (*Jude vs 6 KJV)*

The hybrids born from this unnatural union were no ordinary children.

> *There were giants in the earth in those days; and also after that, when the sons of God came in unto the daughters of men, and they bare children to them, the same became mighty men which were of old, men of renown. (Genesis 6:4 KJV).*

Another thing we know about the Nephilim is that they were giant bullies; tyrants who filled the earth with violence.

> And *God said unto Noah, The end of all flesh is come before me; for the earth is filled with violence through them; and, behold, I will destroy them with the earth. (Genesis 6:13 KJV)*

The Bible describes the Nephilim as "the mighty ones of old times, the men of fame." who left behind a legacy of violence and fear.

> *And God saw that the wickedness of*

man was great in the earth, and that every imagination of the thoughts of his heart was only evil continually." Genesis 6:5 KJV; *And there we saw the giants, the sons of Anak, which come of the giants: and we were in our own sight as grasshoppers, and so we were in their sight.* (*Numbers 13:33 KJV)*

THEOLOGICAL VIEWPOINTS

<u>The Pre-Adamic Race</u>

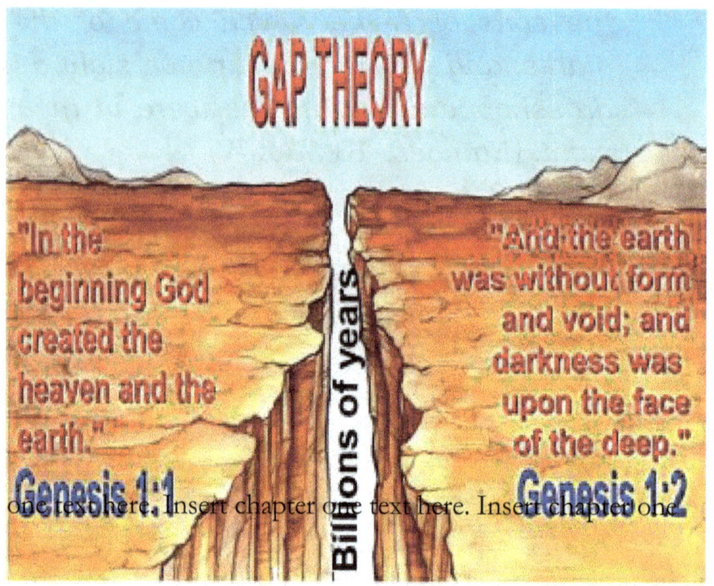

The Gap Theory suggests that there is a gap in time between Genesis 1:1 and 1:2. As such it is believed that human beings existed before Adam and Eve. Supporters of this theory use a few verses in Genesis to substantiate its claim. The Gap theory proposes that creation was completed in *Genesis 1:1 KJV - "In the beginning, God created the heaven and the earth."*

It is believed that it was during this time that

Satan was cast out of heaven and sent to earth where he wreaked havoc destroying the earth and the Pre-Adamic race. This resulted in the earth being without form and void and darkness covering the land as reported in Genesis 1:2. Supporters of this theory believe that from verse 2 onwards is *recreation.*

> *And the earth was without form, and void; and the darkness was upon the face of the deep. And the Spirit of God moved upon the face of the waters....*

They also substantiated their argument in support of this theory by using **Genesis 1:28**:

> *And God blessed them, and God said unto them, be fruitful, and multiply, and replenish the earth, and subdue it: and have dominion over the fish of the sea, and over the fowl of the air, and over every living thing that moveth upon the earth.*

It is believed that the Pre-Adamic race was killed by Satan, and they became demons. In Ezekiel 28: 13-14, it says that before Satan's fall he was in the Garden of Eden, and walked back and forth in the midst of fiery stones. Lucifer became prideful and arrogant and wanted the glory for himself. He said in his heart, "I will be like the most high". So the All-powerful God threw him and his angels out of heaven to the earth. Out of Satan's anger, he flooded the earth killing all of these beings and setting their spirits free. Thus, demons were born.

This belief suggests that after God created the heavens and earth, He also created a race of intelligent beings who were created to worship Him. They had cities, kings, and governments, and probably worshipped God day and night. These physical beings may or may not have looked like us. While there is no evidence in the Bible as it is today to corroborate this theory, be reminded that there are gaps in the writings discovered from which the Bible was compiled.

ANGELS, DEMONS AND FALLEN ANGELS

Differences between Demons and Fallen Angels

Many persons are of the opinion that demons and angels are the same. However, there are several differences between the two beings. Let's look at a few of those differences.

Firstly, demons are the powers of this dark world. The word *demon* is derived from the Greek word *daimōn*, which means a "supernatural being" or "spirit" who is evil or malevolent. Fallen angels, on the other hand, are the spiritual forces of evil in the heavenly realms. Fallen angels are spiritual beings who were expelled from heaven. According to the Book of Jude, these angels abandoned their own homes. There is a big difference between abandoning one's home and being kicked out.

> *And the angels which kept not their first estate, but left their own habitation, he hath reserved in everlasting chains under darkness unto the judgment of the great day (Jude 1:6 KJV).*

The phrase "*abandoned their own home*" could also mean "disrobed themselves". The angels that Jude refers to are certain fallen angels who had committed the sin of disrobing themselves of their celestial bodies and taking upon themselves the bodies of corrupted flesh so that they could have sex with the daughters of men. Jude obviously had these angels in mind, because he associated these angels with the perverted people of Sodom and Gomorrah:

- *...these [angels] he has kept in darkness, bound with everlasting chains for judgement on the great Day.*

- *In a similar way, Sodom and Gomorrah and the surrounding towns gave themselves up to sexual immorality and perversion....(Jude 1:6-7 KJV)*

Notice that Jude says, "*In a similar way*". Then he goes on to describe the sexual perversion of Sodom and Gomorrah. In other words, he says that Sodom and Gomorrah committed the similar sexual sins as these fallen angels. He clearly links the fallen angels with sexual perversion.

The Apostle Paul also differentiated between

these two classes of beings, demons and fallen angels, in Ephesians 6.

> *For our struggle is not against flesh and blood, but against the rulers, against the authorities, against the powers of this dark world and against the spiritual forces of evil in the heavenly realms. – (Ephesians 6:12 KJV)*

In this scripture as in the Book of Jude, we see two beings being referenced:

- the powers of this dark world and
- the spiritual forces of evil in the heavenly realms.

These are both evil spirits and principalities with different ranks and positions in Satan's kingdom. Of note here is the fact that this scripture is not referring to those involved in the war in heaven. The war in heaven depicts Satan's angels as being kicked out of heaven. They did not voluntarily abandon heaven. They were expelled against their own wishes as seen below in Revelation 12.

> *And there was war in heaven: Michael and his angels fought against the dragon; and the dragon fought and his angels,*

> (Revelation 12:7 KJV).

Bishop Tom Brown [2017] differentiated between fallen angels and demons my noting that fallen angels are much more powerful than demons. He noted that Jesus cast out demons. However, in the Book of Jude, we are cautioned about our confrontations with fallen angels.

> *Likewise, also these dreamers defile the flesh, reject authority, and speak evil of [e]dignitaries. 9 Yet Michael the archangel, in [f]contending with the devil, when he disputed about the body of Moses, dared not bring against him a reviling accusation, but said, The Lord rebuke you! – (Jude1:8-9 NKJV)*

Thus, it is proper to rebuke demons but not fallen angels.

Another difference between fallen angels and demons is that fallen angels have their own celestial bodies. They have no need to inhabit bodies but demons seek bodies desperately and if needs be, they will settle for the bodies of animals.

> *And all the devils besought him, saying, Send us into the swine, that we may*

> *enter into them (Mark 5: 12-13 KJV)*

Additionally, fallen angels have the ability to fly and walk, but demons can only walk. Jesus said this concerning demons:

> *When the unclean spirit is gone out of a man, he walketh through dry places, seeking rest, and findeth none. – (Matthew 12:43 KJV).*

Also, angels can become visible and take shapes of humans while Demons desperately need bodies to occupy.

> *Above it stood the seraphims: each one had six wings; with twain he covered his face, and with twain he covered his feet, and with twain he did fly. (Isaiah 6:2KJV)*

Another difference between fallen angels and demons is that angels can eat but demons cannot.

> *Human beings ate the bread of angels; he sent them all the food they could eat. (Psalms 78:25 NIV)*

ANGELS, DEMONS AND FALLEN ANGELS

Can Angels Marry?

Some may argue that *angels can't marry, so the sons of God could not refer to angels because the sons of God were married.* Note carefully the following:

- Only the angels in heaven did not marry. There is no mention of the angels who were cast out of heaven not being able to marry.

- We know from Genesis chapter 3 that Satan had already been cast out of heaven. So the fall of the devil and his angels came before the sons of God came to the daughters of men.

- Fallen angels are already evil, so sexual immorality would not be out of the question for fallen beings.

Jesus' teachings about marriage and the angels in heaven have no bearing on the incident in Genesis chapter 6. Let's look at the passage carefully where Jesus discussed this:

> *Jesus replied, the people of this age marry and are given in marriage. But those who are considered worthy of taking part in the age to come and in the resurrection from the dead will neither marry nor be given in marriage, and they can no longer die; for they are like the angels. They are God's children, since they are children of the resurrection. – (Luke 20: 34-36 NIV)*

Like Luke, Matthew also identifies another key characteristic of angels.

> *At the resurrection people will neither marry nor be given in marriage; they will be like the angels in heaven. – (Matthew 22:30 NIV)*

Therefore, we conclude that angels cannot marry and they will not die. As children of the resurrection, humans will be like the angels because they too can never die nor can they marry.

ANGELS, DEMONS AND FALLEN ANGELS

Angels Bound with Chains

Now we will look at angels that were bound with chains. Who were the angels that were bound with chains in hell? They are mentioned in the book of Jude:

> *And the angels which kept not their first estate, but left their own habitation, he hath reserved in everlasting chains under darkness unto the judgment of the great day. – (Jude 1:6 KJV)*

Some Theologians teach that these angels who are bound with chains in hell are those angels who were cast out of heaven during the war in heaven – the one-third (1/3). If this is true, then they are no longer on the earth because according to this scripture they are bound with chains and kept in darkness. According to Apostle Peter, they are in "hell".

> *For if God spared not the angels that sinned, but cast them down to hell, and delivered them into chains of darkness, to be reserved unto judgment;* (2 Peter 2:4).

The word *hell* found in this passage is the Greek word *Tartarus*, which means prison. If these fallen angels went to prison, then who are the evil spirits that we are fighting with today?

While these two (2) theological viewpoints, The Nephilim's and The Pre-Adamic Race, might be inconclusive as to the origin of demons and fallen angels, the student of demonology must know the varying arguments. They **MUST** understand that irrespective of personal belief concerning the views, one thing is clear: <u>God commands us to confront and cast them out</u>!

> *Behold, I give unto you power to thread on serpents and scorpions, and all over the power of the enemy: and nothing shall by any means hurt you. – (Luke 10:19 KJV).*

Part 2- DEMONIC ACTIVITIES ON EARTH

THE NATURE AND ACTIVITIES OF DEMONS

The 1st, 2nd and 3rd Heavens

There are three (3) heavens mentioned in the Bible, two physical and one spiritual. **The first heaven is the earth and the atmosphere around it**. The second heaven is filled with principalities (fallen angels/wickedness in high places), and the third heaven represents Zion (the throne of God). Throughout the Bible, heaven is the antithesis of hell; a beautiful paradise where God and His angels abide. Let's look at a few scriptures that describe the different heavens.

- *The Lord is in His holy temple, the Lord's throne is in heaven. – (Psalm 11: 4 KJV)*

- *I saw the Lord sitting upon His throne, and all the host of heaven standing on His right hand and on His left. – (2nd Chronicles 18: 18 KJV),*

- *Our Father which art in heaven, hallowed be thy name. Thy kingdom come, Thy will be done in earth, as it is in heaven. – (Matthew 6: 9-10 KJV)*

In the Scriptures, heaven not only refers to Paradise as we understand it but can also mean sky (atmosphere) or outer-space. For example, the expression “birds of the heavens” appears frequently and clearly refers to the sky’s atmosphere, not paradise heaven.

> *Him that dieth of Baasha in the city shall the dogs eat; and him that dieth of his in the fields shall the fowls of the air eat. – (1st Kings 14:11KJV)*

Also, heaven is spoken of as the domain of the sun, moon, and stars.

> *And lest thou lift up thine eyes unto heaven, and when thou seest the sun, and the moon, and the stars, even all the host of heaven. – (Deuteronomy 4:19 KJV)*

So heaven when used in the Bible can refer to either the sky, outer-space, or paradise, depending on the context in which it is used. Even though the Bible generally identifies all three distinct locations (sky, outer-space and paradise) as heaven, it does not teach that they are all the same thing. Additionally, we are told that Jesus passed through the heavens testifies to the existence of different types or levels of heavens.

- *Behold, the heaven and the heaven of heavens is the Lord's thy God. – (Deuteronomy 10:14 KJV),*

- *But will God in very deed dwell with men on the earth? Behold, heaven and the heaven of heavens cannot contain thee. – (2 Chronicles 6:18 KJV)*

- *He that descended is the same also that ascended up far above all heavens, that He might fill all things. – (Ephesians 4:10 ISV)*

- *Seeing then that we have a great high priest, that is passed into the heavens, Jesus the Son of God, let us hold fast our profession. – (Hebrew 4:14 KJV)*

We are given further insight into this subject when the Apostle Paul tells us how he was taken up to the "third heaven" in 2 Corinthians 12:2-4.

I knew a man in Christ above fourteen years ago, (whether in the body, I cannot tell; or whether out of the body, I cannot tell: God knoweth); such a one caught up to the third heaven.... How that

> *he was caught up into paradise, and heard unspeakable words, which it is not lawful for a man to utter.*

Paul identified the *place* as paradise, indicating that the third heaven is paradise. Many theologians believe that Paul was talking about himself and that he was the one who had the experience. If this verse is telling us that there is a third heaven, then it makes sense to believe that a first heaven and a second heaven exist. If God lives in the third heaven, then the first heaven has to be the atmosphere around the earth. If the first heaven is the atmosphere, then the second heaven has to be the "air" or the atmosphere between heaven and our earth. This includes the air that we breathe as well as the space that immediately surrounds the earth. The Bible calls Satan ***"the prince of the power of the air."*** This is the same air where he and his fallen angels live and roam.

> *"And you He made alive, who were dead in trespasses and sins, in which you once walked according to the course of this world, according to* ***the prince of the power of the air,*** *the spirit who now works in the sons of disobedience.* (Ephesians 1: 1-2 NKJV)

Satan is not currently confined to the bottomless pit or the lake of fire and brimstone. He is free to roam in the "air" until Jesus returns in His second coming. After Jesus' return, Satan will then be thrown into the bottomless pit for a thousand years and then eventually into the lake of fire and brimstone at the end of the **1000 Year Millennium Kingdom**. I know we are currently in the second millennium and many persons expected that Satan would have gotten his just reward at the start of the second millennium. However, remember that Psalm 90:4 tells us that 'a 1000years to you are like one day, they are like yesterday, already gone like a short hour of the night" in the eyes of the Lord.

Finally, remember also that Satan rebelled against God and he was cast out of the *third heaven* in the earth.

> *Then war broke out in heaven. Michael and his angels fought against the dragon, and the dragon and his angels fought back.* ***8*** *But he was not strong enough, and they lost their place in heaven.* ***9*** *The great dragon was hurled down—that ancient serpent called the devil, or Satan, who leads the whole world astray. He was hurled to the earth, and his angels with him" (Revelations 12:7-9 NIV).*

The diagram below should help to make this concept clearer.

1st Heaven

This is the earth and the atmosphere around it.

<u>This atmosphere is packed with demons</u>

"For we wrestle not against flesh and blood, but against principalities, against powers, against the rulers of the darkness of this world, against spiritual wickedness in high places."

2nd Heaven

SATAN

The second heaven is the "air" or the atmosphere between heaven and our earth. *(Ephesians 1: 1-2NKJV)*

Fallen Angels (Principalities)

<u>Prince of Persia</u>

"But the prince of the kingdom of Persia withstood me one and twenty days: but lo, Michael, one of the chief princes, came to help me; and I remained there with the kings of Persia."

(Daniel 10:13 KJV)

He wants to be like God so he sets up his throne under God's.

Prince of the power of the air (Ephesians 2:2)

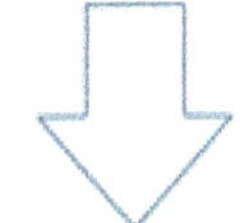

Spiritual wickedness in high places (Ephesians 6:12)

3rd Heaven

Zion – The Throne of God

Paradise

"I knew a man in Christ above fourteen years ago, (whether in the body, I cannot tell; or whether out of the body, I cannot tell: God knoweth such a one caught up to the third heaven."

(Acts 7:55-56, Romans 8:34, 2 Corinthians 12:2, Ephesians 1:20 KJV)

Christ is seated in the third heaven

THE NATURE AND ACTIVITIES OF DEMONS

Home

The home of demons is in the first and second heaven or the "heavenly places" according to Ephesians 6:12.

> *For our struggle is not against flesh and blood, but against the rulers, against the powers, against the world forces of this darkness, against the spiritual forces of wickedness in the* ***heavenly places****. (Ephesians 6:12 NIV)*

Personalities

Demons possess the basic elements of personality. In Luke 8 we can see the demon at Gadarenes demonstrating the faculty of cognition – the act of knowing; perception; awareness. We can see that he knew who Christ was and spoke with Him.

> *When Jesus stepped ashore, he was met by a demon-possessed man from the town. For a long time this man had not worn clothes or lived in a house, but had lived in the tombs.* 28 *When he saw Jesus, he cried out and*

> *fell at his feet, shouting at the top of his voice, "What do you want with me, Jesus, Son of the Most High God? I beg you, don't torture me!"[29] For Jesus had commanded the impure spirit to come out of the man. Many times it had seized him, and though he was chained hand and foot and kept under guard, he had broken his chains and had been driven by the demon into solitary places.[30] Jesus asked him, "What is your name?"* There is no use of the personal pronouns and the demon had a proper name. He said "my name is Legion" (Luke 8:27-30 KJV).

Demons have emotions. They not only know the judgement that awaits them, they also fear it –

> *And there was there an herd of many swine feeding on the mountain: and they besought him that he would suffer them to enter into them. And he suffered them.* – (Luke 8:32).

> *You believe that God is one. You do well; the demons also*

> *believe, and shudder. – (James 2:19 NKJV)*

Demons have will and they can speak and communicate. We see them exercise their volition in Luke 8:31 as they requested of Christ not to command them to go into the abyss.

> *And they begged Him that He would not command them to go out into the abyss* (Luke 8:31).

CHARACTERISTICS

Demons and evil spirits have many names and characteristics. These dark spirits have characteristics and activities that are well-known and documented in the Bible. Let's look at the story in ***Luke 8: 26-33 (KJV)*** *in more detail:*

> *They sailed to the region of the Gerasenes, across the lake from Galilee. When Jesus stepped ashore, He was met by a demon-possessed man from the town. For a long time this man had not worn clothing or lived in a house, but he stayed in the tombs. When he saw Jesus, he cried out and fell down before Him, shouting in a loud voice, "What do You want with me, Jesus, Son of the Most High God? I beg You not to torture me!" For*

Jesus had commanded the unclean spirit to come out of the man. Many times it had seized him, and though he was bound with chains and shackles, he had broken the chains and been driven by the demon into solitary places. "What is your name?" Jesus asked. "Legion," he answered, because many demons had gone into him. And the demons kept begging Jesus not to order them to go into the abyss. There on the hillside a large herd of pigs was feeding. So the demons begged Jesus to let them enter the pigs, and He permitted them. Then the demons came out of the man and went into the pigs, and the herd rushed down the steep bank into the lake and was drowned."

The key points to note from this passage are:

1. The demons were able to speak through the mouth and voice of the demon possessed man. This means it may not always clear whether the demon or the man was speaking.

2. The demons recognized Jesus: who He was, and the power He had over them and possibly some part of their destiny. In other places of the Bible, they asked Jesus, "Have

you come to torture us before the appointed time?" (Matthew 8:29)

3. The demon's effect on the demonized man was to provoke him to abnormal and self-destructive behavior, such as living naked in the wild, inhabiting tombs, and, in Mark's account, cry out and cut himself with stones. (Mark 5:5)

4. The demons gave the man supernormal strength.

5. The ruling demon had a name, Legion.

6. The demons feared going into "the Abyss".

7. The demons desired to go into the pigs rather than the Abyss.

8. The demons being spirits, and therefore not occupying physical space, were able to inhabit the man in large numbers.

9. Perhaps something of their unclean and ghoulish nature may

be deduced from the man's choice to live in the tombs.

10. Demons are perverted beings and are referred to as such in the Scriptures. They are referred to as "unclean spirits" in Matthew 10:1; "evil spirits" in Luke 7:21; "spiritual forces of wickedness" in

Ephesians 6:12 and in Matthew 12:45. Some are more wicked than others. In 1st Timothy we see that they are deceitful and that they have perverted doctrines that men grow to accept.

POWERS

Demons have supernatural intelligence.

They know correct doctrines better than some, if not most Christian, and they also know how to corrupt it.

Now the Spirit speaketh expressly, that in the latter times some shall depart from the faith, giving heed to

> *seducing spirits, and doctrines of devils"; (1 Timothy 4:1)*

> *And it came to pass, as we went to prayer, a certain damsel possessed with a spirit of divination met us, which brought her masters much gain by soothsaying: The same followed Paul and us, and cried, saying, These men are the servants of the most high God, which shew unto us the way of salvation. (Acts 16:16-17 KVJ).*

Even though the woman was speaking the truth, she was possessed by a demon who mocked the Disciples.

Demons have supernatural strength. Their supernatural powers were seen in their: *capability to possess people and have them do extraordinary things.*

> *Who had his dwelling among the tombs; and no man could bind him, no, not with chains* (**Mark 5:3**).

> *And the man in whom the evil spirit was leaped on them, and overcame them, and prevailed against them, so that they fled out of that house naked and wounded* (**Acts 19:16**).

Ability to punish people

> And it was commanded them that they should not hurt the grass of the earth, neither any green thing, neither any tree; but only those men which have not the seal of God in their foreheads. And to them it was given that they should not kill them, but that they should be tormented five months: and their torment was as the torment of a scorpion, when he striketh a man (**Revelation 9:4-5**).

Performance of miracles.

> *That is, the one whose coming is in accord with the activity of Satan, with all power and signs and false wonders (***2 Thessalonians 2:9***).*

DEMON OPPRESSED (DEMONIZED) VS DEMON POSSESSION

DEMON OPPRESSED

It is important that we are able to distinguish between the terms demon oppressed (demonized) and demon possession. The term "demonize" comes directly from the Greek term δαιμονίζομαι (daimonizomai) and is translated as "demon-possessed" or "to be possessed with the devil" depending on the translation being used (Crossroads Bible Church, n.d.). Many churches have different ways of addressing this issue but it is my belief, supported by the lack of evidence in the Bible, that Christians cannot be demon possessed. There is no scriptural evidence that they can be indwelt by demons. However, they can be demon oppressed. Demon oppressed means that their actions can be influenced by demonic or evil spirits.

The word "oppression," comes from a Latin verb meaning "to press down upon." A person who is demon oppressed often feels tired, discouraged and sometimes lethargic, possibly even confused and unable to concentrate or focus appropriately. The Bible does tell us that Christians can be strongly influenced by demons. We see this in 2Timothy 1:7 where young Pastor Timothy was being attacked by a spirit of fear or timidity.

> *For God hath not given us the spirit of fear; but of power, and of love, and of a sound mind (***2Timothy 1:7**).

While fear is an emotion, if unchecked, it can open the door to **the spirit of fear – a demonic spirit** - to oppress the believer. When the spirit of fear enters, it can form a stronghold in the person's life. When this happens, the believer will no longer be operating in faith but their actions will be out of fear. I am sure you know someone who has received a bad report or has some bad news, their initial response was fear. If they do not rebuke or reject this emotion, it can open the door to being oppressed by the spirit of fear. This demon will prevent the Christian from receiving all God has in store for him.

Personal Testimonies

Years ago after accepting the Lord, I found myself struggling with lustful thoughts. This was left unchecked and later led to lustful actions which I later found difficult to break. This is what we refer to as a "*stronghold*" where the enemy fortifies himself in certain areas of our lives. If a believer gives place to the devil, he will come in. The scripture says:

> ...neither give place to the devil.

(**Ephesians 4:27**)

One of my members invited a lady to my church one year. This lady had not left her house in a number of months. She was crippled by fear. She shared that she was deadly afraid of just about everything. Therefore, she locked herself away in her house and refused to leave for any reason. She is now delivered and serving in the church.

DEMON POSSESSION

Demon possession on the other hand, refers to the total inhabitation and control of an available vessel that renders then powerless to control or prevent hedonistic or evil behaviour. The English translation of "demon possession" is used to translate the Greek terms '*daimonizomai*" and "*echein daimonion*". Daimonizomai means "*to be under the power of a demon*". The etymology of the participle daimonizomenos is revealing. The root word daimon refers to demons. The causative stem 'iz' indicates that there is an active cause to the verb daimonizomai. The passive ending 'omenos' indicates the passivity of the subject. Echein daimonion means "to have a demon".

"Demon possession" is not a term used in the New Testament. When one is "demonized", it does not mean that one is owned by a demon. It's a mistake to think that Satan and his demons can own human beings. The New Testament does not convey any such meaning to "daimonizomai" and "echein daimonion". In all 13 occurrences of this term in the New Testament, each case referred to some form of demonization where the demon appears to reside *in* a person. As creatures of God, Jesus Christ controls Satan and his demons, determines their limitations, uses them despite their malicious intent and judges them. God owns everything; Satan and his demons own nothing.

Non-believers can be demon possessed but Christians cannot be indwelt with anything other than the Holy Spirit. This means that non-believers behaviour and speech can be controlled by demonic spirits. We see several examples in the New Testament that testifies to the fact that demons are able to enter and control both humans and beasts.

> *And they come to Jesus, and see him that was possessed with the devil, and had the legion, sitting, and clothed, and in his right mind: and they were afraid (***Mark 5:15***).*

> *For unclean spirits, crying with loud voice,*

*came out of many that were possessed with them: and many taken with palsies, and that were lame, were healed (***Act 8:7***).*

*And his fame went throughout all Syria: and they brought unto him all sick people that were taken with divers diseases and torments, and those which were possessed with devils, and those which were lunatick, and those that had the palsy; and he healed them. (***Matthew 4:24***).*

and a woman was there who had been crippled by a spirit for eighteen years. She was bent over and could not straighten up at all. 12 When Jesus saw her, he called her forward and said to her, "Woman, you are set free from your infirmity." 13 Then he put his hands on her, and immediately she straightened up and praised God (**Luke 13:11-13**).

And, behold, a woman of Canaan came out of the same coasts, and cried unto him, saying, Have mercy on me, O Lord, thou son of David; my daughter is grievously vexed with a devil (**Matthew 15:22**).

After Jesus ascended into heaven, the Disciples

continued to cast out demons by the authority given to them by Jesus.

> *And when he had called unto him his twelve disciples, he gave them power against unclean spirits, to cast them out, and to heal all manner of sickness and all manner of disease* (**Matthew 10:1**).

> *For unclean spirits, crying with loud voice, came out of many that were possessed with them: and many taken with palsies, and that were lame, were healed* (**Act 8:7**).

CASES OF DEMONIZATION IN THE BIBLE

The New Testament has several examples of cases of demonization, where the demon, inside the human being, has **intermittent or complete control of the human body and mind to the extent they experienced physical sickness, disease and disability without any apparent loss of will.** Let's examine a few.

1. THE MAN AT CAPERNAUM (Mark 1:23-27 KJV):

> *"And there was in their synagogue a man with an unclean spirit; and he cried out, saying, Let us alone; what have we to do with thee, thou Jesus of Nazareth? art thou come to destroy us? I know thee who thou art, the Holy One of God. And Jesus rebuked him, saying, Hold thy peace, and come out of him. And when the unclean spirit had torn him, and cried with a loud voice, he came out of him. And they were all amazed, insomuch that they questioned among themselves, saying, what thing is this? What new doctrine is this? For with authority commandeth he even the unclean spirits, and they do obey him.*

2. THE GERASENES MAN WITH A LEGION OF DEMONS (Matthew 8: 28-34 KJV)

And when he was come to the other side into the country of the Gergesenes, there met him two possessed with devils, coming out of the tombs, exceeding fierce, so that no man might pass by that way. And, behold, they cried out, saying, what have we to do with thee, Jesus, thou Son of God? Art thou come hither to torment us before the time? And there was a good way off from them a herd of many swine feeding. So the devils besought him, saying, if thou cast us out, suffer us to go away into the herd of swine.

And he said unto them, Go. And when they were come out, they went into the herd of swine: and, behold, the whole herd of swine ran violently down a steep place into the sea, and perished in the waters. And they that kept them fled, and went their ways into the city, and told everything, and what was befallen to the possessed of the devils. And, behold, the whole city came out to meet Jesus: and when they saw him, they besought him that he would depart out of their coasts.

Other references you can examine are: **Mark 5:**

2-16, Luke 8: 27-38 KJV

3. THE SON WITH CONVULSIONS (Matthew 17: 14-21 KJV)

And when they were come to the multitude, there came to him a certain man, kneeling down to him, and saying, Lord, have mercy on my son: for he is lunatic, and sore vexed: for oftentimes he falleth into the fire, and oft into the water. And I brought him to thy disciples, and they could not cure him. Then Jesus answered and said, O faithless and perverse generation, how long shall I be with you? How long shall I suffer you? Bring him hither to me.

And Jesus rebuked the devil; and he departed out of him: and the child was cured from that very hour. Then came the disciples to Jesus apart, and said, why could not we cast him out? And Jesus said unto them, Because of your unbelief: for verily I say unto you, If ye have faith as a grain of mustard seed, ye shall say unto this mountain, Remove hence to yonder place, and it shall remove, and nothing shall be impossible unto you. Howbeit this kind goeth not out but by prayer and fasting.

Other references: **Mark 9: 17-25, Luke 9: 39-42**

4. **THE MAN WHO WAS MUTE (Matthew 9: 32-33 KJV)**

As they went out, behold, they brought to him a dumb man possessed with a devil. And when the devil was cast out, the dumb spake: and the multitudes marveled, saying, it was never so seen in Israel.

Other references: **Luke 11:14**

5. **THE MAN WHO WAS BOTH BLIND AND MUTE (Matthew 12:22 KJV)**

Then was brought unto him one possessed with a devil, blind, and dumb: and he healed him, insomuch that the blind and dumb both spake and saw.

6. **THE WOMAN WITH THE SPIRIT OF INFIRMITY (Luke 13: 10-17 KJV)**

And he was teaching in one of the synagogues on the Sabbath. And, behold, there was a woman, who had a spirit of infirmity eighteen years, and was bowed together, and could in no wise lift up herself. And when Jesus saw her, he called her to him, and said unto her, Woman, thou art loosed from thine infirmity. And he laid his hands on her: and immediately she was made straight, and glorified God.

And the ruler of the synagogue answered with indignation, because that Jesus had healed on the sabbath day, and said unto the people, There are six days in which men ought to work: in them therefore come and be healed, and not on the sabbath day. The Lord then answered him, and said, Thou hypocrite, doth not each one of you on the Sabbath loose his ox or his ass from the stall, and lead him away to watering?

And ought not this woman, being a daughter of Abraham, whom Satan hath bound, lo, these eighteen years, be loosed from this bond on the Sabbath day? And when he had said these things, all his adversaries were ashamed: and all the people rejoiced for all the glorious things that were done by him.

CHARACTERISTICS OF A DEMONIZED PERSON

A person who is demon-possessed or demonized usually exhibits similar characteristics.

Some of these character traits are clearly described in the Bible:

1. The demon(s) controlled bodily movement, sometimes eliciting bizarre and dangerous behaviour – (**Matthew 17: 14-18, Luke 13: 10-13** KJV).

2. The demon(s) afflicted the individual with disease or a crippling handicap – (**Matthew 9: 32-33, 12:22 KJV**).

3. The demon(s) controlled and disturbed the mind and emotions of the individual - (**Luke 8: 26-35 KJV**).

4. The demon(s) overpowered the human will and rendered it weak of resistance – (**Matthew 17: 14-18 KJV**).

5. The demon(s) expressed themselves audibly using the person's vocal chords in some way – (**Luke 4: 33-35 KJV**).

BODY, SOUL AND SPIRIT

The Temple of the Spirit Man

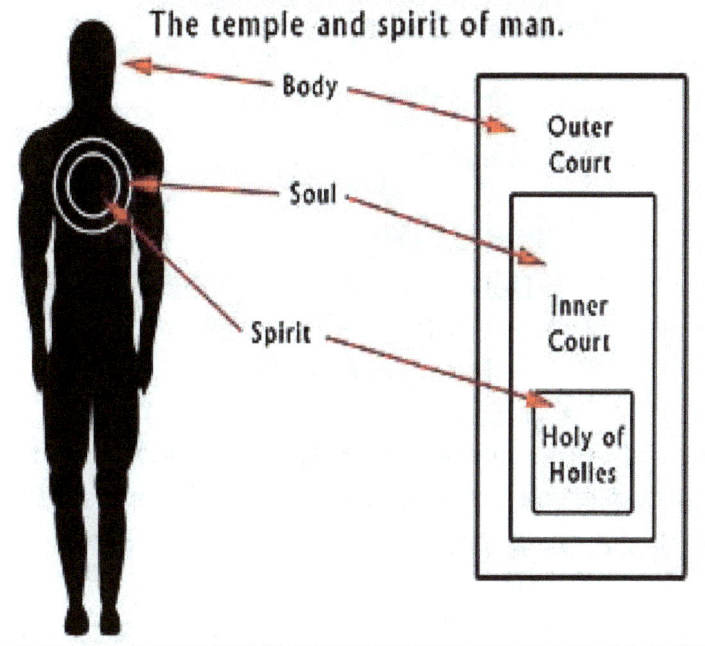

We are tri-partite (three part) beings. We are made up of a body, a soul and a spirit.

> *And the very God of peace sanctify you wholly; and I pray God your whole spirit and soul and body be preserved blameless unto the coming of our Lord Jesus Christ (***1Thessalonians 5:23 KJV***).*

Like the old Jewish Temple, man has a three-part entity with each entity corresponding to the three parts of the Jewish Temple:

1. The Outer Court [*the body*] Exodus 27:9-19

2. The Inner Court [*the soul*] Leviticus 6:12-13

3. The Holiest of All [*the spirit*] Exodus 30:17-21 KJV

The Holy of Holies was the dwelling place of God; it was reserved for Him alone. The Bible says, *"the spirit of man is the candle of the Lord" (**Proverbs 20:27 KJV**).* This may be because the Lord God breathe of Himself in the nostril of man, the breath of life, where He can be found. This breathe came directly from God to man bringing life and light. The spirit of man where God dwells is man's conscience; it enables man to distinguish good from evil.

Additionally, the word of God asks,

> *For what man knoweth the things of a man, save the spirit of man which is in*

> *him? even so the things of God knoweth no man, but the Spirit of God (***1Corinthians 2:11KJV***).*

This shows the deep connection of God with man. You and I are able to know and understand things not because we have a number of degrees but by virtue of the fact that we have the Spirit of God dwelling in us. Also, God knows all things, and He searches all things.

G.H. Pember [2012] in *Earth's Earliest Ages*, suggests the following:

> The spirit of man is the Holy of Holies in the old Jewish temple where the glory of God [*the Shechinah*] dwelt. No one was ever permitted access to this part of the temple except the High Priest, and that but once per year on the Day of Atonement, when he entered it to sprinkle the blood of the sacrifice on the
>
> "Mercy Seat" for the sins of the people.

Christians should be assured that demons **cannot** indwell the *spirit* of a believer because the Holy Spirit resides in them; it is "*is the candle of the Lord"*. However, demons **can** affect the body and definitely the soul (which consist of the mind, the will and the emotions). And as we learnt in the previous chapter, negative emotions left unchecked can develop into major demonic strongholds. Demons love the area of the soul (mind, will and emotions) and generally disguise themselves as personality flaws. They can affect someone mentally and emotionally. Let's look at some examples in the Bible:

Mental Disorders	....	Luke 8:26-35
Spirit Of Fear	....	2 Timothy 1:7
Spirit Of Jealousy	....	Numbers 5:14
Lying Spirit	....	John 8:4)
Murdering	....	John 8:44
Tempting	....	Matthew 4:1
Buffeting	....	2 Corinthians 12:7
Hindering	....	1Thesselonians 2:18
Sifting	....	Luke 22:31
Deceiving	....	2 Corinthians11:3
Corrupting Minds	....	2 Corinthians 11:3
Blinding Minds	....	2 Corinthians 4:4
False Teaching	....	1Kings 22: 21-23, 1Timothy 4:1
Oppressing People	....	1Samuel 18:10
Accusing/Spirit of Condemnation	....	Zechariah 3:1 Revelation 12:10
Divination/False Prophetic	....	Acts 16: 16-18

Christians who are living in obedience to Christ come under satanic attack every day. Can you imagine the fiery darts the enemy throws at us daily, hourly, minutely or even by the seconds? That is why the Apostle Peter encouraged us to resist the devil.

> *Be sober, be vigilant; because your adversary the devil, as a roaring lion, walketh about, seeking whom he may devour: Whom resist steadfast in the faith, knowing that the same afflictions are accomplished in your brethren that are in the world. But the God of all grace, who hath called us unto his eternal glory by Christ Jesus, after that ye have suffered a while, make you perfect, stablish, strengthen, settle you* (**1Peter5:8-10**).

The Apostle Paul gave us the strategies to resist the devil and his demons. He noted that we can resist the devil/demons through perseverance and prayer, putting on the armour of God which is designed to protect the believer from attacks of the evil one.

He said,

> *Finally, my brethren, be strong in the Lord, and in the power of his might. Put on the whole armour of God, that ye may be able to stand against the wiles of the devil. For we*

wrestle not against flesh and blood, but against principalities, against powers, against the rulers of the darkness of this world, against spiritual wickedness in high places. Wherefore take unto you the whole armour of God, that ye may be able to withstand in the evil day, and having done all, to stand. Stand therefore, having your loins girt about with truth, and having on the breastplate of righteousness; And your feet shod with the preparation of the gospel of peace; Above all, taking the shield of faith, wherewith ye shall be able to quench all the fiery darts of the wicked. And take the helmet of salvation, and the sword of the Spirit, which is the word of God: Praying always with all prayer and supplication in the Spirit, and watching thereunto with all perseverance and supplication for all saints; (**Ephesians 6:10-18**).

IF I WERE A DEMON

Use your imagination for a short while and think, *if you were a demon what are some of the things that you would do? Here are a few suggestions*:

- Possess influential persons with the power to change the future of a nation or organization.

- Infiltrate the cultural activities within a nation such as arts (music); the educational system.

- Possess the minds of students and teachers in an effort to influence the future.

These are just a few of the tactics or activities the devil uses to influence people. This is why as Christians we must be filled with God's word and power. If you submit to God and resist the devil he will flee from you for a season.

> *Submit yourselves therefore to God. Resist the devil, and he will flee from you (***James 4:7 KJV***).*

This scripture clearly suggests that there will **always** be devils hanging around you. If you submit to God, they will flee from you. This submission is a daily and continuous action. However, if you fail to submit to God and resist the devil, he will continue to hang around you and may even begin to influence you.

PART 3 – EXPELLING DEMONS

THE BIBLICAL BASIS FOR DELIVERANCE

Deliverance *refers to* **s***alvation, liberation, release, rescue, emancipation and redemption from imprisonment, danger, or evil.* Deliverance in the Old Testament is an act of God wherein, He rescues or save His people who were in trouble or danger from their enemies as found in **Samuel 17:37** and **2 Kings 20:6**. He also rescues His people from the hand of the wicked as seen in **Psalm 7:2; 17:13; 18:16-19 and 59:2** (Butler, 1991)[1].
These deliverances were symbolic representations of the spiritual deliverance from sin that was to come through Jesus Christ in the New Testament.

Deliverance was an integral part of Jesus' ministry· The New Testament mentions Jesus casting out evil spirits fifty-five times, some of which we have looked at in previous chapters. Jesus said,

> *The Spirit of the Lord is upon me, because he hath anointed me to preach the gospel to the poor; he hath sent me to heal the broken hearted, to preach deliverance to the captives, and recovering of sight to the*

> *blind, to set at liberty them that are bruised* (**Luke 4:18 KJV**).

Jesus knew His assignment – to destroy the works of the devil. Destroying the works of the devil is a key element in bringing about deliverance. Deliverance for the captives is synonymous with the granting of freedom for those bound by satanic oppression. It speaks to the undoing of the works of the devil within the lives of individuals. In lay man's term, deliverance is the expulsion of evil spirits from the lives of people who have been demon-possessed or demon oppressed.

In addition to casting out demons, another objective of deliverance is to remove any influences that allow the demon to take control over an individual. For this to be effective the individual must be involved in the process and take responsibility for their actions after the exercise. During Jesus' ministry we saw where He told those delivered to "*go and sin no more*", reiterating the fact that the person has a responsibility to maintain their deliverance.

In today's church, many persons are referred to counselling after the deliverance to continue the process of healing and reformation. Additionally, they are asked to get an accountability partner to ensure they do not revert to old habits that led to the demon possession and given specific Bible verses to use to "*Casting down imaginations, and every high thing that exalteth itself against the knowledge of God, and bringing into captivity every thought to the obedience of Christ;*" (**2 Corinthians 10:5**) as well as to help them "... *Resist the devil,*" (**James 4:7**).

EMPHASIS IN THE GREAT COMMISSION

Modern-day deliverance practices became popular and widespread with the growth of the Pentecostal movement in the 1960s[2]. However, deliverance is emphasized in the great commission.

> *And these signs shall follow them that believe; In my name shall they cast out devils; they shall speak with new tongues*; (**Mark 16:17 KJV**).

The believer, as part of their Christian life and witness, is expected to cast out devils by the authority of Jesus Christ. It is a key sign to one's identity with Christ. It facilitates not just the presentation of the Gospel but the removal of satanic hindrances from the lives of those who so desperately need Jesus. It also demonstrates the superiority of God over the devil and his cohorts.

One day while delivering the message at church, I spotted a man in the service sitting quietly. Let's call it Tom [not his real name]. The Spirit of the Lord revealed to me that Tom was bound and was being controlled by demons. I went over to him and commanded the spirits to get out. He began convulsing and bringing up stuff. By the end of the night, he was delivered and freed from all demon possession. He gave his life to Christ and became a member of my church.

Tom later testified that before he was delivered, he was suffering from a seemingly mental disorder. He shared that he would hear voices in his head and in an effort to quiet the voices, he tried several times to kill himself. He stuffed plastic bags in his mouth and even tried jumping from a moving car. All this stopped when the demon was commanded out of him in Jesus' name. Tom was restored to his right mind and became a mighty man of prayer.

Note that Tom never had to take any medication. Neither did he go to the doctor. Why? Because this was <u>not</u> a natural fight. It was a spiritual one. It was the case of someone who was possessed by the devil and it was being manifested as a mental disorder. This story is similar to the one we read about in **Luke 8:26-35**. Like that '*certain man*' in the Bible, Tom had the devils for long time. They kept him bound until he came into the presence of the Lord while at church. I used the same authority that Jesus gave to His Disciples to expel the demons and set Tom free.

As a Christian, we all have a responsibility to help those who are bound. You are commissioned and equipped to cast out demons. The Spirit of the Lord is upon you to do what Jesus did. But before you do, ensure you are living in obedience to God's word and you are wearing the full armour of God (**Ephesians 6:10-18**).

KEY ELEMENTS IN JESUS EARLY ASSIGNMENT

Jesus was very clear on His reason for Him being on earth. He was given a specific assignment and a limited time in which to do it.

> *For you have the poor with you always, but Me you do not have always* (**Matthew 26:11**).

According to the accounts in the Gospels, Jesus' ministry officially started soon after He was baptised at around the age of thirty. The Gospels also outline the following as Jesus' assignments.

- Jesus came to destroy the works of the devil - (1 John 3:8 KJV).

- Jesus gave His disciples authority over evil spirits – (Matthew 10:1 KJV).
- Jesus came to deliver those troubled by evil spirits – (Luke 6:17 KJV).

- Jesus came to heal those who were sick – (Matthew14:14; Matthew 15:30; Luke 4:39; Acts 10:38 KJV).

- He indicated He would cast out demons until He was glorified – (Luke 13:32 KJV).
- He spoke to the evil spirits and cast them out – (Mark 5:8-9 KJV).

MINISTRY OF DELIVERANCE – A FULFILMENT OF PROPHECY

As we see from the many examples of Jesus going about healing and setting captives free, the early church practiced and was involved in deliverance ministry and it continues today:

- Phillip the Evangelist in Samaria – (Acts 8: 6-8 KJV)
- Paul and Silas in Ephesus casting out a spirit of divination – (Acts 16: 16-18 KJV)

This is necessary because the fight is not against "*flesh and blood, but against the rulers, against the authorities, against the powers of this dark world and against the spiritual forces of evil in the heavenly realms*" **(Ephesians 6: 12).** Demons sought to establish a counterfeit kingdom and were always in opposition to the Kingdom of God. From Ephesians 6: 12 above we see the different hierarchy or ranks of demons in Satan's kingdom as there are different ranks of angels in God's kingdom. Each demon has a different responsibility. Their everyday jobs include:

- Enslaving the human race

- Promoting false faith - (Psalm 106:34-38, Deuteronomy 32:17, 1st Timothy 4: 1-3, 1st Corinthians 10:20 KJV)

- Blinding the mind of people so the gospel doesn't penetrate their minds. (2nd Corinthians 4:4 KJV)

- Oppressing people with illness - (Acts 10:38, Luke 13:11 KJV)

Without fail, demons sought to attack God's people every day using a variety of strategies. Some of which are so subtle, if you are not deeply grounded and connected to your Heavenly Father, you will miss it and attribute it to being personality traits or 'bad luck'. The Bible reminds us that we are to "*be sober, be vigilant; because your adversary the devil, as a roaring lion, walketh about, seeking whom he may devour:...*"(**1Peter 5:8**). How does be try to devour us? Devils try to devour, oppress or possess us by using:

- **Deception** – 2Corinthians 11:4 KJV
  For if he that cometh preacheth another

Jesus, whom we have not preached, or if ye receive another spirit, which ye have not received, or another gospel, which ye have not accepted, ye might well bear with him.

- **Temptation** – Hebrew 4:15-16 KJV

  For we do not have a High Priest who cannot sympathize with our weaknesses, but was in all points tempted as we are, yet without sin. 16 Let us therefore come boldly to the throne of grace, that we may obtain mercy and find grace to help in time of need.

- **Discouragement** – 1Peter 5:6-10 KJV

  Humble yourselves therefore under the mighty hand of God, that he may exalt you in due time: Casting all your care upon him; for he careth for you. Be sober, be vigilant; because your adversary the devil, as a roaring lion, walketh about, seeking whom he may devour: Whom resist stedfast in the faith, knowing that the same afflictions are accomplished in your brethren that are in the world. But the God of all grace, who hath called us unto his eternal glory by Christ Jesus, after that ye have suffered a while,

> *make you perfect, stablish, strengthen, settle you.*

IDENTIFYING AND EXPELLING DEMONS

The presence and nature of evil spirits can be known by two principal methods: discernment and detection.

Discernment

1Corinthians 12:10 lists **discerning of spirits** as one of the nine supernatural gifts of the Holy Spirit. The gift of discerning spirits is one of the most needed gifts in the church today. As a Pastor, I have seen a sharp increase in the number of cases of both demon possession and demon possession individuals. In 1 Corinthians 12 we read that "*the manifestation of the Spirit is given to each one for the profit of all: for to one is given the word of wisdom through the Spirit, to another the word of knowledge through the same Spirit . . . to another prophecy, to another discerning of spirits.*" This is necessary as Jesus Himself instructed us to become "*wise as serpents and harmless as doves*" (Matthew 10:16). This is no natural ability. The gift of discernment is the supernatural ability to detect the spirits that motivates or drives an individual.

Detection

The second method of knowing the presence and nature of evil spirits is by detection. Detection is simply observing the behaviour of a person for abnormalities. When possessed or oppressed by demons, an individual's behaviour changes. As in our story of Tom and the young girl, we see them behaving out of character – being hyper sexual, trying to commit suicide and speaking in unusual tones or "*he tore the chains apart and broke the irons on his feet. No one was strong enough to subdue him*" (**Mark 5:1-20**) are all signs that spirits are controlling the person.

Common Symptoms

Some of the most common symptoms of indwelling demons are as follows:

- Disturbances in the **emotions** which persist or recur.
- Disturbances in the **mind or thought** life.
- Outbursts or uncontrolled use of the **tongue**.
- Recurring unclean thoughts and acts regarding **sex**.

- **Addictions** to nicotine, alcohol, drugs, medicines, caffeine, food, etc.
- Many diseases and physical afflictions are due to **spirits of infirmity.** – (Luke 13:11 KJV).

RELIGIOUS ERROR

Involvement to any degree in **religious error** can open the door for demons as follows:

1. **False Religions** – These include Eastern religions, pagan religions, philosophies and mind sciences

2. **Christian Cults** – All such cults may be classified as bloodless religions: having a form of godliness, but denying the power thereof. – (2nd Timothy 3:5 KJV).

3. **Occult and Spiritism** – Any method of seeking supernatural knowledge, wisdom, guidance and power apart from GOD is forbidden. – (Deuteronomy 18: 9-15 KJV)

4. **False Doctrine** – A great increase of doctrinal errors will be promoted by

deceiving and seducing spirits in the last days. – (1st Timothy 4:1 KJV)

5. **Pocomania, Kumina** – Doors can be opened through palm reading, Horoscope, Astrology – (Isaiah 47:13-15 KJV)

DELIVERANCE TO THE CAPTIVE

Bringing deliverance to the captives is one of the reasons Jesus said the Lord anointed

Him:

> *The Spirit of the Lord is upon me, because he hath anointed me to preach the gospel to the poor; he hath sent me to heal the broken-hearted, to preach deliverance to the captives, and recovering of sight to the blind, to set at liberty them that are bruise.," (Luke 4:18 KJV)*

> Mark 16:17 KJV states casting out demons as one of the first signs of our faith and belief in Christ: *"And these signs shall follow them that believe; in my name shall they cast out devils; they shall speak with new tongues...*

When ministering deliverance there are some key things you need to ensure are in place before you start. Firstly, you are to ensure you are:

Are saved

And there were seven sons of one Sceva, a Jew, and chief of the priests, which did so. And the evil spirit answered and said, Jesus I know, and Paul I know; but who are ye? And the man in whom the evil spirit was leaped on them, and overcame them, and prevailed against them, so that they fled out of that house naked and wounded. – (Acts 19: 14-16 KJV)

These men weren't saved and was seeking to manifest an authority that was <u>not</u> given them.

<u>Know your God-given authority through the word</u>

It's your God-given responsibility to cast out demons.

> *And he ordained twelve, that they should be with him, and that he might send them forth to preach, And to have power to heal sicknesses, and to cast out devils: (Mark 3: 14-15 KJV)*

> *Behold, I give unto you power to tread on serpents and scorpions, and over all the power of the enemy: and nothing shall by any means hurt you. (Luke 10:19 KJV)*

> *And these signs shall follow them that believe; in my name shall they cast out*

> *devils; they shall speak with new tongues; They shall take up serpents; and if they drink any deadly thing, it shall not hurt them; they shall lay hands on the sick, and they shall recover. (Mark 16:17-18 KJV)*

Be Compassionate

Compassion and not showmanship is what we need.

> *And Jesus went forth, and saw a great multitude, and was moved with compassion toward them, and he healed their sick. – (Matthew 14:14 KJV)*

Take control of the atmosphere

Give open command(s) restricting other demons from operating, thus making deliverance difficult. If possible, have someone worshipping softly. Sing victory songs and songs about the blood of Jesus.

Identify and bind the strongman

How can one enter into a strong man's house, and spoil his goods, except he first bind the strong man? And then he will spoil his house. – (Matthew 12:29 KJV)

Command demons to go

After conducting the initial interview and listening to the person's spiritual and emotional history, encourage a renunciation or confession by the person of any involvement in activities or sins that give the sprit legal right to be in their body. Then command the spirit out.

> *And Jesus rebuked him, saying, Hold thy peace, and come out of him. (***Mark 1:25 KJV***)*

It is important for us to issue a command when we are casting out demons. Note that Jesus didn't ask or suggest or even implied that the demons go. He commanded, which is an authoritative statement that leaves no question as to what action is exception of the recipient. You too must take that posture during deliverance. The devil will only respond to that level of confidence.

WORKING AS A DELIVERANCE MINISTER/WORKER

Jesus sent His disciples out two by two to heal the sick and cast out demons. It is better to work with others. In any case, **never get into a counselling or deliverance situation alone with a person of the opposite sex.** Satan will send people for counselling who later accuse ministers of sexual misconduct and other inappropriate things. It you were alone with that person and they accuse you, it is your word versus theirs. You can lose your reputation and ministry this way - through false accusations – so be intentional about putting specific boundaries in place to protect your ministry and your reputation.

Synergy among team members is very important. The deliverance minister who leads the team, comprising of other deliverance ministers/workers, must ensure the team relationship is in good order. Additionally, everyone on the team **MUST** be watchful. They **MUST** watch and pray daily.

Humility is another trait that must be associated with a deliverance minister/worker. Practice humility and forgiveness so that Satan cannot gain an advantage over you.

Be united – where there is unity between brethren, Christ is present and commands His blessings.

Be thorough. Identify what areas of demonic influence are in the person's life: by listening to them by asking questions and by listening to God and the gifts of the Holy Spirit. Some things are obvious, others require revelations from God. Do not depend on the demons themselves for information. Although Jesus once asked the demon his name, you generally don't need to. Jesus did not ask each of the thousands of demons in that man what their names were (Mark 5L9 KJV).

Identify demons by what they promote. Thus demons of fear, lust, deception, pride, anger, violence, and so on can be commanded to leave using just those names. For example, you can say, "You spirit of fear, come out in Jesus name!" or "I command you spirit of infirmity to loose her now in Jesus' name!"

STEPS TO DELIVERANCE

Excerpt from *Pigs in the Parlour* by John Black [1982]

The person receiving deliverance should do the following:

1. **Be honest with himself and with God** if he expects to receive God's blessing of deliverance.

   Ask God to help you see yourself as He sees you and to bring to light anything that is not of Him (Psalm 32:5, 139: 23-24).

2. **Be humble.** This involves recognizing that one is dependent upon God and His provisions for deliverance (James 4: 6-7).

3. **Be opened**. It also involves a **complete openness** with God's servants ministering in the deliverance (James 5:16).

4. **Be repent.** Repentance is a determinedly turning away from sin and Satan (Amos 3:3). One must **loathe** his **sins** (Ezekiel 20:43).

5. **Be watchful and renounce any connection with darkness.** Renunciation is the forsaking of evil. Renunciation is action resulting from repentance (Matthew 3: 7-8).

If one has to repent of a religious error, he will need to completely renounce it by destroying all literature and items associated with that error (Acts 19: 18-19).

6. **Be Forgiving -** God freely forgives all who confess their sins and ask for forgiveness through His Son (1John 1:9). He expects us to forgive all others who have ever wronged us in any way (Matthew 6: 14-15). Willingness to forgive is absolutely essential to deliverance (Matthew 18: 21-35). In prayer, ask God to deliver you and set you free in the name of Jesus (Joel 2:32). *"For if ye forgive men their trespasses, your heavenly Father will also forgive you: But if ye forgive not men their trespasses, neither will your Father forgive your trespasses."* – (Matthew 6: 14-15 KJV).

7. **Be communicative.** Communicate with the Holy Spirit and ask Him to guide you.

8. **Be engaged in warfare prayer -** Warfare prayer and warfare are two separate and distinct activities. Prayer is towards God and warfare is towards the enemy. Our warfare against demonic powers is not fleshly but spiritual (Ephesians 6: 10- 12, 2nd Corinthians 10: 3-5).

Use the weapons of submission to God, the

blood of Jesus Christ, the Word of God, and your testimony as a believer (James 4:7, Revelation 12:11, Ephesians 6:17) to war against the enemy. Christ cannot fail! He is the Deliverer (Mark 16:17, Luke 10:19, Psalm 18:2).

HOW TO TREAT DEMONS

Matthew 9:33- 34 –Cast out: to eject, drive out, pluck (dumb demoniac), thrust out, expel (the dumb demoniac)

Matthew 17:18 – Rebuked: censure, admonish

Matthew 1:34- Suffered: to send forth (sick or possessed with demons)

Luke 11:14 - Casting: put out, send away (demon that was dumb)

Ephesians 4:27 - Place: location, condition (give no opportunity to the Devil)

James 4:7 – Resist: oppose, withstand (resist the Devil)

1 John 3:8 – Destroy: loosen, break up, put off (destroy works of the Devil)

As you can see from the Scriptures, we forcefully drive demons out of Christians but we do not argue with demons.

Luke 9:1 says we have power and authority (mastery, superhuman force, violence, control) and **Luke 10:7** says the demons are subject (subordinate, obey) to Christians.

STUDY OF THE BLOOD OF JESUS

The Old Testaments told of rites and bloody sacrifices of the law to redeem the people from their sins, which foretold the shedding of the blood of Jesus Christ. The New Testament told of dignity and perfection of the blood and sacrifice of Jesus Christ. The following Scriptures will give you an overall view of what the Bible says about the blood of Jesus:

Genesis 4:10;	***Numbers*** 19:4;	***Hebrews*** 9:7-14, 10: 19-
Exodus 12:7, 13, 22-23,	***Joel*** 3:21;	22, 12:24, 13:20;
24:6, 8, 29:12, 16, 20-21;	***Romans*** 3: 25-26, 5:9;	***1st Peter*** 1:2, 19-22;
Leviticus 4: 6-7, 5:9, 7:2,	***Ephesians*** 1:7;	***1st John*** 1:7, 5:7-8;

8:24, 17:11;		***Revelations*** 12:11

HOW TO TREAT DEMONS

Counselling

In many cases, if the individual is not counselled, the devils will return through ignorance and a negative mindset. Therefore, I strongly recommend collaboration between counselling and deliverance.

> *My people are destroyed for lack of knowledge: because thou hast rejected knowledge, I will also reject thee, that thou shalt be no priest to me: seeing thou hast forgotten the law of thy God, I will also forget thy children.* (**Hosea 4:6 KJV**)

> *Afterward Jesus findeth him in the temple, and said unto him, Behold, thou art made whole: sin no more, lest a worse thing come unto thee.* **(John 5:14 KJV**)

> *And ye shall know the truth, and the truth shall make you free.* (**John 8:32 KJV**)

Part 4 – MAINTAINING FREEDOM

MAINTAINING YOUR DELIVERANCE

1. Total commitment to Christ - (Matthew 22:37, John 12:26 KJV).

2. Obey God instead of engaging in tradition to please Him – (Hebrews 4: 9-11 KJV)

3. Regularly study and draw life from the Word – Psalm 119:9, 11, 105, 165, Psalm 1: 1-3, 2nd Timothy 2:15 KJV).

4. Be accountable to someone that watches over your life – (Hebrews 13:7, 17 KJV).

5. Put on and wear the full armour of God – (Ephesians 6:10-18 KJV).

6. Pray in all circumstances: thanksgiving, praise and worship – (1st Thessalonians 5:17, Psalm 100 KJV).

7. Keep fellowship with spiritually minded people – (Hebrews 10: 24-25 KJV).

8. Regularly make positive confessions of faith in God's ability and power which is

working in you – (Mark 11: 22-24, Romans 10: 8-10 KJV).

9. Don't be yoked with unbelievers – (1st Corinthians 6: 14 – 7:1 KJV).

10. Memorize and understand your position in Christ – (Galatians 2:20 KJV).

11. Deal promptly with sin – (1st John 1:9 KJV).

12. Forgive and let go – (Matthew 6: 14-15, 7: 1-2 KJV).

13. Ensure your Christian walk is in order, or restore it to divine order – (1st Timothy 3: 3-13, Ephesians 5: 18-33, 6: 1-4 KJV).

14. Submit yourself to God – (James 4:7 KJV).

A SPIRIT FILLED LIFE IS THE ONLY WAY TO STAY FREE.

- *And they were all filled with the Holy Spirit. – Acts 2:4 KJV*

- *Then Peter, filled with the Holy Ghost, said unto them,... - Acts 4:8 KJV*

- *And when they had prayed, the place was shaken where they were assembled together; and they were all filled with the Holy Ghost, and they spake the word of God with boldness. – Acts 4:31 KJV*

- *Brother Saul, the Lord,even Jesus...has sent me so that you might regain your sight and be filled with the Holy Spirit. – Acts 9:17 KJV*

- *But Saul... filled with the Holy Spirit, fixed his gaze upon him, – Acts 13:9 KJV*

The Real Holy Ghost Baptism:

Pray in tongues

For if I pray in an unknown tongue, my spirit prayeth, but my understanding is unfruitful. (1 Corinthian 14:14 KJV)

But ye, beloved, building up yourselves on your most holy faith, praying in the Holy Ghost... (Jude 1:20 KJV)

SAMPLE PRAYERS

Pray this prayer with authority out loud

Prayer before Deliverance

Dear God, in the name of JESUS, according to Romans 10:9, I confess with my lips that JESUS is Lord, and in my heart, I believe that He is raised from the dead. According to Luke 13:3, I repent of my past sins, and I admit and confess that I have sinned (name). I believe that you are faithful and just to cleanse me from all unrighteousness. I call upon You, Lord JESUS, to cleanse me from all sin and unrighteousness by Your blood (1st John 1:7); and as Your Word says in Romans 10:13, everyone who calls upon the name of the Lord will be saved.

I confess, repent and ask forgiveness of occult practices such as (witchcraft, fortune telling, horoscopes, astrology, water witching, etc.). I renounce all occult and satanic practices and I break all curses associated with those occult practices. According to Galatians 3:13, Christ purchased our freedom [redeeming us] from the curse [doom] of the law [and its condemnation] by [Himself] becoming a curse for us, for it is written [in the Scriptures], cursed is everyone who hangs on a tree (is crucified) – Deuteronomy 21:23.

I confess, repent, and ask for forgiveness of all sins listed in Deuteronomy 27 and 28 and I break the curses associated with these sins. I confess, repent and ask for forgiveness of my iniquities and my father's iniquities according to Leviticus 26:40, and I break the curses associated with these iniquities.

I break and loose myself from all evil soul ties with my mother, father, brothers, sisters, spouse, former spouses, former sex partners, etc. Lord Jesus, I forgive my mother, father, brothers (name), sisters (name) and ___________ and anyone else who has ever hurt me. Matthew 6:15, 18:21, 22, 35; Luke 11:4 (Lord's Prayer).

I break and loose myself and my family from all curses that have been and are being placed upon me and my family: curses of witchcraft, physic thoughts or prayers, ungodly intercessory prayers and words spoken in anger, and I return these curses to the sender(s) sevenfold and bind them up by the blood of JESUS, in JESUS' name, Amen.

Sample Deliverance and Bondage Breaking Prayers

Below are some sample deliverance and bondage breaking prayers. Please understand that there may be other factors involved in any given bondage, such as, if you are trying to break a soul tie with a rock group, but refuse to get rid of any CDs that you have from them. If you are suffering from deep bondage in these areas, it may be a good idea to have a strong believer present in case the demons begin to manifest.

<u>Breaking Soul Ties</u>

Heavenly Father, I confess and repent of the sin of ____________ (name the sin which caused the evil soul tie, such as adultery or fornication), and I ask that you forgive me of this sin. [Now is a good time to destroy or get rid of any physical gifts or other objects that could hold the soul tie together, such as a gift given in adultery, etc. Anything that could hold the bond together between you and that person.]

In the name of Jesus, and by the power of His blood, I now renounce, break and sever all unholy soul ties formed between ____________ (name the person) and myself, through the sin of ___________ (name the sin which caused the evil soul tie, such as adultery or fornication).

I now command any evil spirits which have taken advantage of this unholy soul tie to leave me now in the name of Jesus!

(Repeat this prayer if you have more than one evil soul tie to break.)

Renouncing Ungodly Vows

Heavenly Father, I repent and renounce the vow I made to ___________ (name the demon or person, or even god that you made the vow to) to perform ___________ (describe what the vow entailed). I realize that it was foolish and rash on my behalf, and I ask that you will forgive me and release me from the bondage that this vow has brought me under. In the name of Jesus, and by the power of His blood, I now renounce, break and nullify the vow to ___________ to perform ___________, and I confess that I am released from this vow and its bondage in Jesus' name.

I now command any evil spirits which have taken advantage of this unholy vow to leave me now, in the name of Jesus!

(Repeat this prayer if you have more than one unholy vow to break.)

Renouncing Involvement with Unhealthy (demonic) Music

Heavenly Father, I confess that I used to listen to unhealthy demonic music. I ask that you will forgive and cleanse me from this sin. In the name of Jesus, and through the power of His blood, I now renounce, break and sever all soul ties that have been formed between myself and the unhealthy music (name specific songs and artists/groups if possible) I used to listen to and enjoy, as well as any soul ties formed between myself and the artists and groups (name them specifically if possible) and demonic influences that have produced these unhealthy songs and music.

In Jesus' name, I also renounce, break and nullify any curses that I may have come under as a result of listening to the unhealthy music I used to listen to and enjoy. In the name of Jesus, I now command all evil spirits to leave me that have taken advantage of these soul ties I have just renounced. In the name of Jesus, I also renounce and command any evil spirits that have taken advantage of any curses that I have come under as a result of listening to unhealthy music to leave me now in Jesus' name! I also renounce and command any evil spirits that have entered me through my listening to this unhealthy music to leave me now in the name of Jesus'!

Breaking Generational Curses

In the name of Jesus, I confess the sins and iniquities of my parents (name specific sins if known), grandparents (name the sins if known), and all other ancestors.

In the name of Jesus, and by the power of His blood, I now renounce, break and sever all cords of iniquity and generational curses I have inherited from my parents, grandparents, and all other ancestors. And I break and sever all unholy soul ties formed between myself and my parents, grandparents, and all other ancestors.

In the name of Jesus, I now loose myself and my future generations from any bondages passed down to me from my ancestors, and I command any evil spirits which have taken advantage of these cords of iniquity, generational curses and unholy soul ties to leave me now in the name of Jesus!

References

Brown, T (2015). *Origins of Demons.* http://tbm.org/origins-of-demons.html

Butler, T.C. (Ed.). (1991). Entry for Deliverance, Deliverer. Holman Bible Dictionary. https://www.studylight.org/dictionaries/eng/hbd/d/deliverance-deliverer.html.

Hammond, F & I. (2018). *Pigs in the Parlour.* https://archive.org/details/PIGSINTHEPARLORByFrankIdaMaeHammond/page/n223

Hunt, S. (May 1998). Managing the demonic: Some aspects of the neo-Pentecostal deliverance ministry. Journal of Contemporary Religion, 13 (2): 215–230. doi:10.1080/13537909808580831.

Pember, G.H. (2012). Earth's *Earliest Ages (5th ed.).* Defense.

www.ingramcontent.com/pod-product-compliance
Lightning Source LLC
LaVergne TN
LVHW020031170826
845678LV00001B/218

* 9 7 8 9 7 6 9 6 7 0 8 9 1 *